A Deep Breath and Twelve Foot Pruners

Theresa Harrell Hatfield

WestBow
PRESS
A DIVISION OF THOMAS NELSON

WestBow Press books may be ordered through booksellers or by contacting:

WestBow Press
A Division of Thomas Nelson
1663 Liberty Drive
Bloomington, IN 47403
www.westbowpress.com
1-(866) 928-1240

Because of the dynamic nature of the Internet, any web addresses or links contained in this book may have changed since publication and may no longer be valid. The views expressed in this work are solely those of the author and do not necessarily reflect the views of the publisher, and the publisher hereby disclaims any responsibility for them.

Certain stock imagery © Thinkstock.
Any people depicted in stock imagery provided by Thinkstock are models, and such images are being used for illustrative purposes only.

All scripture quotations used in this book are from the *Holy Bible,* The Scofield Reference Bible, Copyright 1909, 1917; copyright renewed, 1937, 1945 by Oxford University Press, Inc.

ISBN: 978-1-4497-1791-9 (sc)

Library of Congress Control Number: 2011929266

Printed in the United States of America

WestBow Press rev. date: 6/8/2011

To my wonderful son,

DJ

You make me proud to be your mother and it is my prayer that
you continue to seek God's guidance in your life's journey.
Thank you for bringing joy to my life on so many levels.

To my awesome husband,

David

You are my best friend and you complete me in every
way. Thank you for your love and encouragement.
God knew exactly who I needed to take life's journey
with and I wouldn't change one moment.

Contents

The Situation   1

The Application   21

The Invitation   43

The Situation

Chapter One

Have you ever awoke in the morning, realizing that you have a new day ahead of you, and instantly wondered with eager anticipation what excitement the day might hold? Like the first day of your long awaited vacation, or you decided last year on your birthday to spend your next birthday spoiling yourself and today is that day. Well this was not one of those mornings. It was a Saturday and on the agenda was a family gathering. Not a special event or holiday, just a good ole family gathering. I didn't wake up with any expectation of having a thought-transforming experience. In fact, on Saturday I do my best to avoid anything that requires a lot of brain power.

I do recall noticing the beauty of the day. The sky was Caribbean cruise blue and there was a slight breeze. Intermittently a white cotton ball of a cloud would appear and float across the sea of blue as if it was on a timeless journey. It was the type of day that is good to cloud watch. Yes, I said cloud watch. You lie on a blanket in the yard and watch the clouds. Oh, they are not just your normal every day clouds, not at all. You get to watch the dinosaur clouds, the lion clouds, the valiant knight on his steed or the anything-your-imagination-wants-to-see clouds. Okay, let me get my head out of the clouds and back to the real story of the day.

The anticipation of anything occurring on this day that would require me to draw from a vast array of senses to the point of later causing me deep self-reflection was not on my list. Getting the food prepared to take to the family pitch–in and confirming that it was edible was my first goal. Arriving with all the prepared dishes upright was next. Somehow when in transit food tends to travel in the opposite direction of the vehicle. A close eye must be kept on the jigglers or they will inch their way to the edge of the plate as if toying with the idea of jumping to see if they actually bounce on the fuzzy car mats as they do on the ceramic tile of the kitchen. I know the answer, but they are never satisfied with my efforts to enlighten them. Lastly enjoying a relaxing day with the family was the extent of the necessities for this Saturday. No pressure, no deep thought, no stress of the everyday hustle and bustle. It was just a beautiful spring day to be spent with family.

We loaded and secured the food in the car. Did the dummy check; if you are not familiar with what a dummy check is, that is when you take one last look or walk through to make sure you didn't forget anything. Then we loaded and secured ourselves into the car, counting noses as the dummy check making sure no humans are left behind. My family that cohabitates with me consists of my awesome husband, David, our fabulous son, DJ (yes, I am very partial to my family) and me. Each one of our noses was accounted for so we were ready to head to Hazelwood, Indiana with an estimated trip time of 25 minutes.

Chapter Two

David and I met in grade school but it was not until junior high that Cupid worked his magic. Looking back we know it was God using divine intervention but at 14 I am pretty sure we didn't know or really care what that meant and Cupid is a little more romantic sounding. We attended school and church together. Our youth outings were great because we got to 'date' before we could actually date. David's parents were our youth leaders so we spent a lot of time together. Not just David and me but us and his parents. We dated through high school and college. I do not know how, maybe it was the divine intervention thing again, but I knew in eighth grade that David was the one I would marry. On May 20, 1983, we were married only three weeks after David's college graduation. Yes, we were young and high school sweethearts. There were people who said we wouldn't make it. I am truly blessed to be married to my best friend forever-or in the world of technology, my BFF. Sharing so many of our early years has provided lots of memories with David's family. On this day we were headed to his childhood home where his parents, the best in-laws ever, still live.

Hazelwood is a rural community and their house is amidst cornfields and lots of several-hundred- year-old trees. Since this is the place where David grew up he often has the look of reflection when we drive to their home. I can predict that he will look at certain landmarks as we are driving and I know he is reflecting on a memory or just acknowledging that whatever it is, a tree or a barn is still there just as it has always been. I find myself doing the same. And DJ, although consciously unaware that he does it, is turning his head and looking for those familiar sites. There is a sense of comfort in taking time to reflect on these things. Today was no different.

Chapter Three

We traveled the familiar roads and I am sure we chatted as families do. It was just a regular jaunt from our house to theirs. At least that is how I remember it until we approached the bridge.

About a quarter of a mile before you get to their house, there is a concrete bridge. There is a small creek that flows under the road, thus the need for this bridge. This is one of those memory spots of David's. He has many fond childhood memories of trekking down to the bridge in hopes of finding some treasure that had been discarded or swept to that spot by the spring rains. Usually there was nothing new, but occasionally there might be a find, even if it was just crawdads burrowing into the soft moist edges or enough water flowing to send a leaf floating with the wonder of just how far it would go.

As we approach the bridge I know that David will slow down. It is a habit that over time has cemented itself as a tradition. Usually our gaze only sees the new erosion that has occurred or a few small fish that have found a temporary feeding ground. David starts to slow down. Families who spend a lot of time together tend to take on the same actions or routines; almost as if our heads are all connected, the three of us begin to rotate our heads to look to our right.

As David approached this spot, he slowed down and actually stopped as to take a lingering look; this was different. We continued turning our heads to the right, nothing out of the ordinary but there was some water flowing which we noted was a good thing with the surrounding crops. We were sure that there were probably some fish, but we could not see clearly through the flowing ripples. Then as our robotic heads were once again in sync, we turned our attention to the driver's side and what we saw was completely out of place. Lying half way down the bank as if it had been tossed by a moving vehicle was a suitcase. The expression of surprise was unanimous. Why would there be a perfectly good latched suitcase lying on the creek bed? It was almost hidden from sight if you were just driving by and not purposely looking for something. We mused over its placement, torn between investigating it and its possible contents. There was a car approaching from behind so our decision to continue on was made for us. David started moving and we began the last quarter mile of our journey. We were all very quiet; our chattering had changed into an eerie silence. We pulled into the driveway, still not saying a word but I am sure each one was secretly wishing that we had further investigated the mysterious suitcase.

Chapter Four

Trying to put the suitcase out of our mind, we carried the carefully prepared and packaged dishes in to the house. All were upright and each jiggler accounted for. The kitchen was a bustle with the final meal prep, the family room was filled with the sounds of pro golfers – Wii pro golfers, and the newest generation was emanating the sounds of childhood play. We immediately were engulfed with family greetings and busying ourselves with the last phase prior to the attack of the buffet. Our minds were much occupied. We were having a variety of family conversations, catching up on recent events, and processing all of the great smells of the food that was permeating through the house. Somehow through all of this we each knew that *the suitcase was beckoning.* We somehow unconsciously agreed not to mention our find to anyone else so periodically during the meal prep, the three of us would inconspicuously huddle as if trying to determine our next play. Which later we realized was exactly what we were doing. *Why would someone put it there? Did it fall off of a truck when someone was moving?* We would then disburse and go back to our tasks of readying the meal.

The rest of the family arrived so the twenty-plus of us filled our plates and disbursed to assorted tables to enjoy the meal and family time. *But the suitcase kept beckoning.* Occasionally our eyes would meet and we knew what each of us was thinking. *What could be in it? It was in really good condition to just throw it away in a creek.*

The unconscious agreement still existed; we had not shared our secret with anyone else. We each had our own reason for keeping our secret. Perhaps they would laugh at us and think us stupid to be so caught up as we were with a discarded suitcase. Were we? Or what if it did contain a treasure? Did we want more people in on the find? After all, there were three of us who knew about it and that was already cutting into the profit. Or had one or more of them seen it on their way to the house and they were going through the same thought process? Who would get to it first?

We ate our food, going back for seconds and yes, probably thirds. After all, a Hatfield pitch-in beats any smorgasbord restaurant anywhere. We caught up with the ongoings of the family, had a lot of laughs and made some memories. Family is so important and the best thing we have on this earth. But even with all of these calming distractions *the suitcase kept beckoning. What if it does have something of value in it? Did someone commit a robbery and stash the goods until they felt the coast was clear? Could we help the police solve a crime?*

Chapter Five

It was the time after the meal where choices are made. Some choose to clean up the meal carnage, some choose to nap, and some choose to do anything except the first choice. I went into the kitchen to help with the cleanup but unbeknownst to me at the time, David went to his dad's garage to look for a long pole or something that could reach the suitcase from the side of the road. *After all, we didn't know what was in it so we didn't want to tamper too much with the evidence or mess up any fingerprints and DNA.*

Clean up was done and I went outside to see where David and DJ were. You know, so we could form another huddle to talk because *the suitcase was beckoning louder.* It didn't take me long to find David because he actually found me to ask me if I wanted to take a walk. I didn't have to ask him where we were walking; I knew we were going straight for the bridge.

DJ was already waiting in the front yard. David and I met up with him and as the three of us walked towards the road David turned and hollered back to those on the deck that we would be back, we were taking a walk. Then he knelt down to pick up, yes you guessed it, a very long pole. It was a twelve foot tree pruner to be exact. Complete with the hook and pull mechanism. It was easy to hide the pole as we vacated the yard due to all of the parked cars. So we started our journey towards the bridge with a twelve foot pole in hand. *The suitcase was shouting at this point.*

We trekked eastbound single file with the pole on our right side so we could conceal it from passing cars. After all, why are these three people walking down the road with a tree pruner? Did their truck break down and were afraid someone might steal the pruner as they went for assistance? In the rural areas people are apt to stop and ask if you need help. That is a part of America that is sadly missing in today's culture, but on this day we were not looking to reinstate it. So we walked and talked keeping the pole as hidden as possible.

We decided that we would inspect it from the road and top of the creek bank. We had watched enough crime shows that our crime scene investigation skills were now kicking in. We knew we needed to check for any insects on or around the suitcase. This could indicate a body or something unpleasant that might be secured in the suitcase. We needed to check the area around it as well for other items or things that seemed out of place for the creek bed. We needed to cautiously sniff for any odd smells. I am not exactly sure what we were supposed to smell for but I guess we would know if we smelled it.

Chapter Six

Today the bridge seemed farther away than on previous walks. *Would the suitcase still be there? Did the person who stashed it there already come back for it? Were they hiding and waiting for the unobserved moment that they could retrieve it? Were we messing up their plans? Were we being totally ridiculous about the entire situation?* After what seemed like a day's journey, we arrived at the bridge. We peered cautiously over the railing, it was still there just as we had left it; staring up at us, taunting us with its mystery.

We changed our focus and listened for approaching cars. All was quiet except for *the suitcase beckoning to us.* The three of us stared down at the brown case. It was a hard shell suitcase that appeared to be in excellent condition. No visible scratches or dents. It was closed and latched; just sitting there as if it was packed and ready to go on a journey. We began conversing and again pondering why it was there. It was so out of place.

It was time to look at our options and develop our plan. We had come too far to stop. We had to know what was in that suitcase. David was sure that he could unlatch it from atop the bridge with the pruning mechanism thus keeping us all safe from whatever might jump from the suitcase or present to us a bad situation.

We studied the area around the suitcase from afar. We did not see any other out of place objects. There were not any insects lingering on or near it. We did not see any odd patches of discolored grass or dirt. We leaned and peered under the bridge as far as we could see and found nothing out of the ordinary. David told us to stay put and to hold onto the pruning pole. He walked across the road to view the opposite creek bed, leaned over the railing to view under the bridge and found nothing odd. The suitcase was the only out of place item.

We still didn't have a specific plan. We wanted to make sure we were not overlooking some important detail so David decided that he wanted a closer look at the suitcase. So as DJ and I held the pruning pole tightly we watched him as he made his way partially down the creek bed, nearer to the beckoning suitcase. He cautiously leaned and looked around it as best as he could. It seemed unscathed and harmless. He squatted down and peered under bridge able to see completely under it from this angle and again found nothing unordinary.

He joined us back at the rail and structured the plan. David would wield the pruning pole thus putting himself closest to the unknown and between it and his family. As always, taking the role of the great protector, David instructed me to hold onto the long rope that worked the mechanism in order to keep it out of the way. DJ was to stand by me with his hands free so he could be ready to react instantly as needed. Each of us had our assignment. If we had thought that synchronizing our watches would have made us any more prepared, we would have set them.

The suitcase was staring at us and we knew that we needed to make our move. We were clear about our roles and ready to put action to our plan; ready to find out what mystery was being concealed by the foreboding suitcase.

Chapter Seven

David took the pole from DJ and me. His big, strong hands held it tightly as he began to maneuver it over the railing. It was twelve feet long and a bit awkward to control but he carefully guided it towards the suitcase. He was going to have to extend the majority of its length down at an angle while maintaining a tight grip. Keeping the pole steady and away from the grips of gravity was going to be a challenge. We did not want to connect with the suitcase too hard because that might make it move further away from us. Connecting too lightly would not provide the power needed to pop the latches. It was definitely going to require some skill and David was the man for the job.

He carefully started lowering the pole towards the first latch. It wobbled a bit up and down and then side to side picking up momentum like a pendulum. He pulled the pruning pole back towards him and rested it on the rail. It seemed like such a simple task. There we were just inches away from finding out what was inside, so close and yet so far away. The suitcase was enjoying our struggle and it seemed to be smirking at us. We regrouped and David was ready. Once again he started lowering the pole over the rail and towards the suitcase. His hands were steadier on this try and as if the pole and left latch were magnetic they connected. He applied a little pressure and victory was achieved as the latch popped open. The three of us let out the breath that we had unknowingly been holding for quite some time. One latch was free and nothing out of the ordinary had occurred. We looked at each other with our eyes full of various emotions. There was relief and accomplishment mixed with apprehension and anticipation. We could feel each other's thoughts and knew we were too far into our plan and we had to finish. There was not going to be any latch undone, any suitcase unopened. Taking a deep breath David grasped the pole and started its descent one more time. We stood breathlessly as he was again successful. He connected with the second and final latch. He pushed slightly and once again victory was obtained as the latch effortlessly popped open. The suitcase stared up at us. We had violated its security and it knew we would soon know the secret that it held.

There we were, just one more pole use away from knowing what was in it. It was time for the answer that we had been seeking for so many hours. It was time to put an end to all of the mystery and find out what was in the suitcase. Odd, but this just seemed to bring more questions to the situation. Each of us seemed to have created our own list of twenty questions that we had not shared yet. *What if it is the goods from a robbery? Are we tampering with evidence? If it is something of value, what do we do with it? Is the person who stashed it here watching us right now to see what we do? Are they ready to take back what they feel is their property? What if it is a bomb? Set to go off when the lid is lifted? What if it contains a weapon used in a crime? What if a snake or wasps were able to infiltrate it while it was left unattended? What if it is full of money? Is opening it worth the risk of finding out?* It was a major family moment; we considered our options and within the blink of an eye we knew that we could not stop now. We had to proceed with what we started. We did agree that if we found anything questionable that we would stop and call the police. So with our hearts pounding and our breath held we once again turned our full focus on to the suitcase as it sat there patiently waiting.

We took our places again and eye contact was made that we were in agreement. David, who had gained a lot of experience over

A Deep Breath and Twelve Foot Pruners

the past minutes in maneuvering the pole, once again steered the pole down towards the suitcase. This time we would have to get the pruner hook just right so he could lift the lid with enough upward momentum to open it all the way. It would not be good to start opening it and have the lid slam shut. With caution and his recently acquired expertise he guided the pole to connect with the suitcase. He was able to catch the edge of the lid on the first try. With one quick yet gentle move he was able to lift the lid up, up, up and then with a little bit of force he pushed it back so that the lid fell as it should, exposing the inner chamber of ominous suitcase. As the lid was pushed and falling backward, I jumped backward as well, somehow thinking that would help to save us or at least save me from whatever was exposed. I am not sure how David and DJ reacted as my eyes were fixed upon the suitcase.

Chapter Eight

The moment was finally here. We were staring at the suitcase. It was opened wide inviting the world to see what it had to offer within its confines. The three of us stared down at it unable to take our eyes off of it. We stood there staring down at its openness. We stood there staring down at its emptiness. Yes, it was completely empty. Standing on the bridge in the outdoors with the sounds of water rippling, birds chirping and nature at its finest on this beautiful day, you could have heard a pin drop. The inside of the suitcase was just as tidy as the outside. The lining was unscathed and unscarred. It seemed to be staring up at us in complete silence. We had conquered it and it now seemed lifeless.

We were happy to be safe but somewhat disappointed. It would have been exciting to find something in it yet we just were not sure what we wanted to find. Although we had been able to find out its contents we still did not know how it had arrived at this destination. It seemed to be a nice suitcase and not likely that someone had intended for it to end up on a creek bank to be battered by the weather or curious souls. So while we had solved the mystery of its contents, we knew that we would never solve the mystery of its journey to Tudor Road. Not knowing where it came from we decided to leave it as we found it. Perhaps the person who misplaced it would retrace their trip and locate their possession. After all, it might have just fallen off of a truck that morning and its loss had not been discovered yet.

With the pruning pole in our hands we started back to the house. We were not the least bit concerned about concealing it on the return trip. As we walked we took turns recapping the events that had unfolded over the course of the day; each of us recalling snippets that had taken us on a roller coaster ride of emotional responses. We laughed about how we were so consumed by the suitcase and intrigued by its unknown contents. We shared relief that we did not find something criminal or fall unsuspectingly into someone's nasty prank. The best realization was that despite the fact that we had not found anything of material fortune or anything to generate notable fame, we had made a memory and that made the whole experience priceless.

We arrived back having only been gone for about thirty minutes; it seemed that it should have been longer. David took the pruning pole to return it to the garage. The family was sitting on the deck and could see David with the pole. We were going to have to come up with something to tell them that would explain the three of us taking a walk with twelve foot pruners. DJ and I loitered outside of the garage while David put the pruners away. The three of us started this adventure together and there is safety in numbers; safety in the hope that the family would not think that the three of us were crazy, two maybe but not three. David joined us and as we approached the deck we could feel all eyes upon us. As if they had been practicing their parts we heard a chorus of "What were you doing with the pruning pole?" ring out. The three of us gave knowing glances to each other. We knew we had to give an explanation. I know that each of us tried to think of a logical reason we could present for having taken the pruning pole for a walk but we were not thinking quickly. We had exhausted our thinking capabilities on the suitcase.

Knowing the consequences of telling the truth would lead to embarrassment and endless teasing, it was our only option. So we proceeded to explain. We started out just trying to give them the

"Cliff Notes" of the story, but realized if we were going to share it then we might as well make it as real to them as it was to us.

It was actually quite refreshing to us because as we were telling it, one of the family would interject a question like "What if there had been money in it?" Which indicated that they were thinking the same way that we had: Was there potential for there to be something of value or mystery concealed in the suitcase? Our embarrassment soon passed allowing us to give them the details, thus it took us quite a while to recap the story. In the end, they shared in the disappointment that we did not find anything of value and also shared in the relief of not finding something gruesome. They laughed with us, not at us. I am sure that each one of them would have done the same thing if they had seen the suitcase first.

The Application

Chapter Nine

I have shared this story with a few people since that day and reflected back to it a few times. Each time I still chuckle. I think about how silly some of it, no actually most of it, was. A lot of time and effort was put forth by us to see what that suitcase held, but I would not trade one second of it. It was one of those moments that you cannot plan; it just happens and takes you on a journey that you did not know what the outcome would be. Full of curiosity, laughter, mystery, planning, and fear of the unknown – just like the journey of life.

When we are living life and the events it brings we are usually so into the specific moments that we cannot see the bigger picture. I believe that we can learn from all of our life experiences, whether they are good or bad. Taking and applying the good and bad is what builds our character. The suitcase continued to beckon to me long after that day. Once again I was becoming consumed by a suitcase but this time I knew what was in it, nothing. What could I possibly need to gain from this experience that would cause me to keep reflecting upon it? So practicing what I preach I realized that I needed to look at this suitcase journey a little bit closer. I needed to try to see how I could learn from it. I needed to look for a spiritual application for my life since it seemed to keep beckoning. It seemed like an odd prayer at the time but we are instructed to ask God for anything, so I did. I asked Him to show me how this suitcase, that continued to beckon to me, could enrich my life. Well, He did not waste any time in His response. I have other requests that I have been waiting on for years, like can I please wake up and be a size four? So He started revealing to me how this is an example of how we, I mean, I live life.

I am always wishing I had more time. There are so many things that I need to do and a long list of things that I want to do. My life tends to feel cluttered and never able to get it all done. I end up carrying around a lot of baggage full of guilt and frustration, just to mention a couple of items. If I did not have to eat, I would have more time to get things done and then I would be closer to a size four, but that is not being realistic.

Back to the beckoning suitcase or actually I should say God's beckoning. I believe that He put that suitcase in a ditch on a country road to enrich my life. The family thinking that we were crazy on that day pales in comparison to the possible consequences of that statement. But I have learned that God can use anything to make His point. He used everything from rain to talking donkeys in biblical times to get people's attention. So using a suitcase to get my attention is not out of the question. I am just thankful that it did not speak audibly.

So as I began to pray and ponder about this suitcase journey, it dawned on me that during our life journey we all carry a suitcase, metaphorically speaking of course. We do not realize it at the time, but we are constantly picking up things as they cross our path and packing them away. As I thought more about that idea, I began to realize that there are a variety of suitcases that we can choose to carry. God allows us to select our suitcase. Of course He will assist us in picking it out but we have to ask for His help. So what kind of suitcase should we carry? What suitcase would God prefer us to carry?

Chapter Ten

I am a list maker. Lists are what keep me functional. I even have lists for my lists. I especially like the note pads that are sticky on the back, these are direct from heaven; I can make a list and stick it anywhere. When I am preparing to pack for a trip, I start a list. It could be a long trip or just an overnighter. It does not matter what the length of the trip will be, I know that a list needs to be made so that I know what to pack, but more specifically so I know which suitcase or suitcases I will need to use to most efficiently hold the items on the list. Choosing the right suitcase is important for any journey.

There are the soft, canvas duffle bags. These bags conform to allow for pushing and shoving so you are able to fit lots of items into them. Its structure allows for it to be deformed and reformed creating more storage space. The items placed inside are usually not well kempt. Organization of the items is limited and any clothing will definitely need the benefits of a good iron. Non-clothing items can easily be damaged due to its flimsy structure. A busted bottle of shampoo could spoil the entire trip. This is the luggage selected by most pre-teen boys since they do not usually pack shampoo.

Another type of suitcase to consider are the suitcase sets that have zippers that go north, south, east and west. They have so many hidden compartments that when you start to pack for your trip you find something you forgot to unpack from the last trip, hopefully it is not the dirty underwear compartment. These types of cases provide excellent organization. Somehow they compel us to fill every compartment, which can lead to over packing. The over packing is easy to disguise due to the handy rollers; you do not realize how much the suitcase might actually weigh until you have to lift it in or out of the trunk. And if the wheels break, how will you maneuver all of your stuff?

Ah, yes, the toiletry bag. This is the prime piece of luggage; the suitcase that you pack all of the items that you cannot possibly live without – the makeup, the hair products, the toothpaste, the toothbrush and the deodorant. But be afraid; be very afraid when putting all of these necessities into one bag because this is always the bag that will take a different flight than yours. I found this out when I went to Arizona. I landed at my destination but my toiletry bag went to Florida. Who knew it preferred the ocean? This bag is designed to hold the liquids and solids that give you the presentable persona of a clean life. It is lined with a heavy duty plastic just in case something might expectantly leak. It has several separate compartments so you can sort your items for better overall protection. Zip up the shampoo and other liquids in one area and put your make up in another zip pouch so never the twain shall meet. Besides being roomy for bottles and odd shaped items, it also has special pouches for jewelry and other bling items that we must have to make our outward appearance top notch. We consider these our necessities of the trip; they allow us to create who we want to be seen as on the outside.

There is still one more suitcase that I need to mention, the type that we found, the hard shell, gorilla proof suitcase. I remember a television commercial several years ago where one of these suitcases was placed inside a cage with a gorilla. The gorilla jumped on it, threw it on the ground and against the bars of the cage. He did his best to try to destroy it but despite his efforts it remained unscathed. This was to convince the customer that whatever was inside would be protected no matter how the suitcase was handled. These are the model T's of the suitcase clan. These cases provide a sturdy box format to pack your belongings. Not a lot of frills and there are definite limitations on how much you can pack into them. But in the event it is thrown from a moving truck or accidentally dropped into a gorilla cage, your items will be completely safe. They are not that common and are very easily spotted on the luggage carousel at the airport.

So having thoughtfully reviewed the types of suitcases that we can carry in our travels, I realized that God was definitely giving me a spiritual application through all of this. He was providing me with an opportunity to reflect upon my life's journey and to look at the baggage in my life.

Chapter Eleven

The canvas duffle bag has been a part of my journey. I have made an attempt to collect everything that I can. Not caring if it is going to benefit me or even considering that it might hurt me. Not paying attention to what it is or where it is in the bag. I cram and push things into the bag trying to fill each corner thinking that this will somehow create a stable foundation for everything that gets put in it. This shoving can easily cause the seams to stress and even rip. When the time came that I needed something, it was not an easy process to dig and feel around for the item. Unclear of what was hindering my search, persistently shoving and pushing to make a chaotic situation even worse. Finally needing to dump the entire contents to find the thing I needed. It was there, but it sure would have been nice to reach in and just pull it out instead of having to dig through the chaos.

Paul's letters to the church at Corinth were written to provide guidance on Christian conduct. The church body was having issues. Imagine that, even back in Paul's day the committees could not agree on the color of carpet. Paul set out to provide the church with guidelines to help them correct the wrong that was occurring. In Corinthians 14:33 he writes "For God is not [the author] of confusion, but of peace, as in all churches of the saints." That is pretty clear; God doesn't create confusion in our lives. So I fully expected the next verse to read "Theresa allows Satan to create confusion and steal her peace." God wants us to collect all of the knowledge, lessons, experiences, and events of our life. He wants us to glean from these to find our talents and spiritual gifts. Wisdom comes from applying what we have learned but He wants us to be able to reach in and pull out what we need from Him when we need it. Just as Paul's letters were clear in instruction on providing order and structure for the church, God wants us to be able to simply reach and find Him without having to dig through the chaos. I need to be rid of the duffle bag in my life: perhaps it would like to be sent to Florida.

Chapter Twelve

Since chaos is not a good choice, then organization must be the key. I am a very organized person. I find that things go so much smoother with organization. So that must mean that a better way to be organized for a trip would be with a suitcase set. After all they are the ones with all the zippers and compartments that have a place for everything and everything in its place. I have been a victim of these tempters as well. I happily go along in life collecting everything knowing that I can carefully secure it in its own special compartment. This seems like a logical step in the right direction. This makes me organized by tucking everything away into the perfect compartment. This is true until I need something. It then becomes a guessing game because I cannot remember which special and secure compartment I placed it in or even which case in the set. I now have so many cases with compartments and zippers that I'm not letting God guide me, I am too busy searching for the answers that I know I have stashed away. Unfortunately this is probably one of the most popular of the luggage family. We allow ourselves to think that we have it all together. We think we are the big dog leading the pack. But what we are actually doing is making our personal relationship with Christ too complicated. We feel a sense of having all of the right stuff exactly where we need it. We are falsely prepared to conquer whatever comes our way. I have spent a lot of precious time undoing zippers. I keep looking in the next compartment and then the next becoming frustrated because I know it is there somewhere because I know that I put it there. It becomes all about me being dependent upon myself to solve whatever I am up against. I spend my time trying to prove that I have it under control instead of looking to the One who truly does.

There is one lady in the Bible who I am positive owned one of these suitcase sets. Her name is Martha. She is portrayed as a homemaker and from what is recorded in the New Testament, I do believe that she was a very organized woman. She had a servant's heart and desired to provide the best accommodations and nourishment for her family and friends. I am sure she would have really enjoyed having a suitcase set with all of those compartments. She could have packed it for one of her brother Lazarus's trips. Busying herself with the need to fill each compartment with something that he may or may not need and not realizing that Lazarus would not know which one to look in for what he needed. She would be so caught up in wanting to make sure that he had everything that she would not realize he might not easily find the one thing when he needed it. Why do I think this? Because on one specific occasion when Jesus came to visit she was so caught up in the busyness of making sure the food was prepared, that the guests were tended to and all of the little details that she lost sight of the importance of the visit, the importance of the one whose presence she was in. Martha became irritated that Mary didn't share in her burden of preparation. She became so caught up in her own organization of the preparations that she actually complained to Jesus about her sister, Mary. Martha complained to Jesus that Mary was not helping. While she was busy, Mary was just sitting. I cannot relay the story better than the scripture does. In Matthew 10:39 – 40 we read where the complaint to Jesus is voiced, "And she had a sister called Mary, which also sat at Jesus' feet, and heard his word. But Martha was cumbered about much serving, and came to him, and said, Lord, dost thou not care that my sister hath left me to serve alone? Bid her therefore that she help me." It is our nature as children to try to get our siblings in trouble with our parents, but Martha went right to the top. I do not think that when we are told in Hebrews that we can boldly approach the throne of grace that this is what God intended. Martha's complaint did not go unnoticed; in fact Jesus took the opportunity to teach her and the generations after a very basic lesson. He addresses the situation in Matthew 10:41–42, "Martha, Martha, thou art careful and troubled about many things: But one thing is needful: and Mary hath chosen that good part, which shall not be taken away from her." Jesus had to remind Martha that she needed to refocus on what was truly needed. I have often been like Martha, blindly seeking things to make a situation better instead of focusing on the One. The Martha line of luggage is quite burdensome and I definitely need to avoid it.

Chapter Thirteen

Shampoo and conditioner, check; razor and lotion, check; deodorant, toothpaste and tooth brush, check; make up, check – double check. When packing my toiletries bag I mime my way through the daily routine of getting myself ready to face the world. It is my recommendation when doing this mime that you lock yourself in the bathroom to prevent the possibility of being observed. That way you do not have to explain what you are doing to your loved ones in order to convince them that you are not losing it and when you are interrupted you lose your train of thought which could lead to forgetting something very important. I carefully pack the items in the toiletries bag, making sure the lids are all tight, securing the items as best I can to avoid opening my bag when I arrive at my destination to find a mess of gunk and goo.

I realize that on a daily basis I put a lot of thought and preparation into grooming my outward appearance but often I do not fully attempt to be spiritually groomed on the inside to face the world. Spiritual grooming, just like physical grooming, takes constant effort but unlike physical grooming the results are not always immediately visible. Being physically groomed can give us confidence that we look our best, that we are acceptable and that we are ready for whoever we might meet. Being spiritually groomed gives us the confidence in the fact that we do not have to face anything or anyone that comes our way alone. We should have a daily spiritual grooming checklist that might go something like this: Spent time in prayer being thankful, check; spent time praying for others, check; asked Him for His continual guidance today, check; read His word, check; took time to be still and listen for Him, check. It is so easy to get caught up in the physical necessities of our daily routine easily forgetting that we need to include God on that necessity list when we start to pack our day. If we are not careful, we will find a mess of gunk and goo when we arrive at our destination.

Perhaps Eve had forgotten to do her spiritual grooming. Even though she lived in the perfect place, had a perfect husband and flawless skin does not mean that she did not have to groom, physically or spiritually. She was human and physical grooming is a just a part of life. Being human also means that she had a soul and she needed to provide it with spiritual grooming. God provided a wonderful world for Adam and Eve to live in and there was only one stipulation, they could not eat of the tree of the knowledge of good and evil. Imagine living in a beautiful garden and having all that you needed and only one rule to follow. Spending your days stress free, enjoying all of God's creations and literally walking and talking with God. It sounds so easy to us. But just as we are tempted daily, Adam and Eve had temptation as well. I suspect that Eve had become so comfortable with her perfect life and the daily routine of it that on this particular day she decided that she was all prayed up. She thought that it would not make a difference this one time to skip her prayer time. After all she could always do it later and she was more interested in taking her morning walk. So as she is walking, feeling the warmth of the morning sun on her shoulders and not having a care in her perfect world she comes upon a serpent, a serpent that had been waiting for her and waiting for a day just like this. The conversation recorded In Genesis 3 between Eve and the serpent is only five verses long. (Genesis 3:1-5) " Now the serpent was more subtil than any beast of the field which the Lord God had made. And he said unto the woman, Yea, hath God said, Ye shall not eat of every tree of the garden? 2)And the woman said unto the serpent, We may eat of the fruit of the trees of the garden: 3)But of the fruit of the tree which is in the midst of the garden, God hath said, Ye shall not eat of it, neither shall ye touch it, lest ye die. 4) And the serpent said unto the woman, Ye shall not surely die: 5) For God doth know that in the day ye eat thereof, then your eyes shall be opened, and ye shall be as gods, knowing good and evil." The serpent spoke to her, she replied, and then the serpent spoke again. That was it. That simple verbal exchange was all that it took for Eve to be deceived by Satan. She completely turned her back on all that God had provided for her and her family. I do not know for sure if on this particular day Eve had forgone her spiritual grooming, but she certainly was an easy target. Her actions as a result of this encounter created a mess of gunk and goo for her, her family and the entire human race.

The toiletries suitcase is one that we must not get too attached to. We must avoid focusing more on our physical grooming instead of our spiritual grooming, for even just one trip, because the results can be devastating in our life journey. I have to remember daily to make room for the true necessities of life.

Chapter Fourteen

That brings me to the last suitcase in this journey, the hard shell, gorilla proof suitcase. If you remember, that is how this journey started. This is a suitcase that does not offer any frills. It does not offer the conformability of the duffle bag. It does not have lots of compartments. It does not provide the security of a plastic lining. It is very basic in its structure and detail. Even though it does provide durability with its hard outer shell making it quite capable of withstanding lots of stress and bumps, overall it would not be the suitcase of choice for travel.

This suitcase reminds me of Mary, the mother of Jesus. We read in the scriptures that she was highly favoured and blessed among women. (Luke 1:28) "And when the angel came in unto her, and said, Hail, thou that art highly favoured, the Lord is with thee: blessed art thou among women." Now think about that, an angel tells you that the Lord has been watching you and He wants to tell you how wonderful HE thinks YOU are. That certainly had to knock her sandals off, but before she could possibly have recovered the angel really gets on a roll. She finds out that she has been chosen to give birth to the Saviour of the world. The book of Luke records the conversation between the angel and her about these upcoming events.

I am sure her head was spinning trying to process the information that the angel was delivering to her. The magnitude of the honor and responsibility had to be overwhelming. The reality of being unmarried and pregnant meant that she would be shamed and shunned. She was espoused to be married to the love of her life. This young girl who was on the threshold of beginning her adult life was going to experience things that she could not explain to herself, much less to others. The weight of the world had to be bearing down on her. Her level of stress had to be a C5, you know, Chocolate Level 5. The intensity of a tornado is rated by the Fujita Scale which goes from F1 to F5 with the latter being the most intense. So I rate stress by the Chocolate Scale and Mary had to be experiencing C5 level. But God had picked Mary and that was all that she needed to know. Her response is a true reflection of who she was and why she was chosen. (Luke 1:38) "And Mary said, Behold the handmaid of the Lord; be it unto me according to thy word."

Mary knew that God would protect her and her family. She knew that God would be her hard shell to protect her and withstand whatever this journey might bring. She knew that she had everything that she needed, a heart for God on the inside and His unfailing protection on the outside. Mary did not have to dig through the chaos of a duffle bag to try to find what she needed. Mary did not need to busy herself with trying to locate things in a luggage set. Mary did not fear that her toiletries bag would have a mess of gunk and goo waiting for her.

Mary had journeyed through her young life knowing that she only needed a personal relationship with God to fulfill her needs. God saw her commitment of faith and honored her with an extraordinary mission. She willingly accepted what was set before her and she never looked back. Her walk with God was pure and simple. (Luke 2:19) "But Mary kept all these things, and pondered them in her heart." This verse occurred after the birth announcement and after the shepherds had visited the manger. So a lot has transpired from when the angel first appeared to Mary. But I think that this verse gives us the most insight about Mary's character. She pondered in her heart;

she thought things over very carefully letting her heart guide her instead of her head. Pondering allows time so as not to react quickly; to use self control; to be patient. Mary was able to seek God and His wisdom in any situation and be patient to wait upon His timing.

She had God and that made her content. She was not concerned about the situation or what the outcome would be. This does not mean that she was perfect. She was human and I am sure there were moments of doubt but she knew who was in control. She did not allow herself to be distracted by things or the clutter that life can bring. She was not perfect but her suitcase of life was. It was basic, just like the one we found. It was sturdy, just like the one we found; and it was empty, just like the one we found.

Chapter Fifteen

So as I mentioned earlier, I kept reflecting back to the day that we found the suitcase and the events that transpired. I felt God could teach me something from it and He has definitely done that. He provided an experience for me that involved so many things that are a part of who I am.

Family is definitely a priority in my life and I am blessed to have a wonderful husband and son. God allowed this memory to include them. The three of us were able to work together in harmony. When the situation was intense, we leaned on each other and kept each other's best interest at the forefront. Have I mentioned that I have a wonderful husband and son? We could have easily become irritated with each other but love was stronger and conquered.

Thinking of ways to solve problems and situations is another part of who I am. I remember as a young girl how I wanted to be Nancy Drew when I was reading all of her mysteries. Or be part of a crime solving duo like Shaggy and Scooby Doo. Well, God made me wait a long time but I finally got to experience a little bit of what it was like. He gave me my own mystery to solve. Granted, I still do not know how or why the suitcase was left at the creek bed but I am content that we were able to solve the biggest mystery which was finding out what was inside of it. As I have heard it said many times, 'it is the thrill of the hunt'.

I enjoy laughter. It is a big part of who I am. I enjoy laughing, making people laugh and hearing the laughter of others. Have you ever had one of those unexplainable laughs where the silliest thing sets you off and you literally cannot stop laughing? The tears are streaming and your legs are crossed for fear of unwanted streaming and you become consumed with laughter. Those are the best laughs. Once you finally gain control you feel as if you just returned from a much needed mini vacation. I learned a long time ago that if I could laugh and laugh at myself it made life so much better. God provided lots of laughter around the suitcase story. We were not laughing much during the actual investigation but since then there has been plenty of it. Each time I look back I think of how silly the three of us must have looked and I usually LOL as we say now. (That is Laugh Out Loud for those of you who have avoided learning the abbreviated forms of communication these days.) Of course each time that we share the story with family and friends there is always plenty of laughter.

Chapter Sixteen

In reflecting on the events of that day I see that a lot of memories were made with my family, a desire that goes all the way back to childhood was manifested, and a situation that would continue to bring laughter to me and others was provided. These are three very basic things. God has allowed me to see how cluttered my life has become with things that really do not matter.

My luggage rack contains too many suitcases. Not just one each of the various types, but more like one of them in every color. I know that I am guilty of carrying them all, not at the same time, but depending upon what my spiritual meter is at the time determines which one I grab. I have collected a lot of unnecessary stuff on my life journey. I have packed it away with the idea that I am going to have to depend upon it someday. God has shown me that I do not need all of that stuff. He has shown me that collecting stuff just creates a lot of heaviness and burdens in my life that robs me of my joy. He has brought me back to the realization that He is truly all that I need. He wants me to depend upon Him and allow Him the opportunity to supply my every need.

I asked God to show me a spiritual application and He has. Now I must ask Him to help me apply it. This is the hardest part because I have allowed myself to lose focus in the journey of life and clutter it with stuff. I must get back to the basics. One of my life passages is about that exact idea. (Proverbs 3:5, 6) "Trust in the Lord with all thine heart; and lean not thine own understanding. 6) In all thy ways acknowledge him, and he shall direct thy paths."

You may think it odd that God allowed a suitcase to be placed in a creek bed for me to find, and you may think it even odder that I chose to write about it. But I believe that God uses all types of situations to get our attention. He knows us and what makes us tick. He knew that suitcase would beckon to me and He allowed it to actually speak to me. So ask yourself these questions, which suitcase are you carrying? Do you know what is in it? *Can you hear it beckoning to you?* Perhaps you should take a deep breath and even a twelve foot pruner pole if you need some extra security, and open your suitcase. You might be surprised at what you have collected over the years and how little you really need. I suggest you try getting back to the basics.

The Invitation

The Best Chapter

Perhaps you are at a loss on how to get back to the basics. All of us experience life's journey with its ups and downs. We have been on cloud nine with feelings of love, joy and hope. And we have sunk into the bottomless sea of hate, sadness and depression. These are all normal, human emotions; the very emotions that God created us with and that He allows us to experience. He never told us that being a Christian would take the ups and downs from us; He simply promised us that He would share our burdens with us and not give us anything that we could not handle – as long as He was included in our daily walk.

Life's journey is not easy for anyone. Each day is a new adventure for each of us. We are never prepared for what the next text message or phone call might bring, be it good or bad. The unpredictable cannot be avoided but having Christ in our lives makes it bearable. When we are totally dependent upon our unpredictable emotions, we leave ourselves wide open to react emotionally. Even receiving good news and letting emotions take over can consume us negatively. Have you ever seen someone be recognized for an achievement and instead of being humble and thankful they choose to indulge in self-pride and let their emotions feed their ego? God does not want us to be boastful; He wants us to do our best but know that without Him we truly are nothing.

God loves us and He knows all about life and its ups and downs. He loves us despite our selfishness and wants a relationship with us. He wants to walk with us on our life's journey. He wants to pick us up and carry us when the journey gets rough and we grow weary from it.

If you do not have a personal relationship with Christ, then you are walking this journey alone. You are packing your suitcases daily without hope of ever emptying them. God does not want us to be burdened down. As I said, it is all about getting back to the basics.

There is a basic journey that will lead you right to Christ. There is nothing that you need to pack or prepare to take on this journey. You just need to come as you are and you will see how much luggage you are burdened with and how He can lighten your load.

There are just a few steps in this journey. Start by telling Him how you feel. That you know you are a sinner and that you are burdened by the things in your life. That you do not want to depend upon self any longer but you want Him to come into your life to guide you, to be with you in ALL areas of your life. That you want Him to forgive you for all of your past and that you want Him to help you create your new future serving Him. That you want to live for Him now and have the security of knowing that you will live eternally in heaven with Him when your life's journey has ended.

The verses that follow go along with starting this new journey. The Bible is your road map for this new journey and God is your guide. I encourage you to read your map daily and check in with your Guide, this will provide you with all of the basics that you need for what your life's journey may bring.

The Romans Road

- Romans 3:10 As it is written, there is none righteous, no, not one.

- Romans 3:23 For all have sinned, and come short of the glory of God.

- Romans 5:8 But God commendeth his love toward us, in that, while we were yet sinners, Christ died for us.

- Romans 5:12 Wherefore, as by one man sin entered into the world, and death by sin; and so death passed upon all men, for that all have sinned.

- Romans 6:23 For the wages of sin is death; but the gift of God is eternal life through Jesus Christ our Lord.

- Romans 10:9-11 That if thou shalt confess with thy mouth the Lord Jesus, and shalt believe in thine heart that God hath raised him from the dead, thou shalt be saved. For with the heart

man believeth unto righteousness; and with the mouth confession is made unto salvation. For the scripture saith, whosoever believeth on him shall not be ashamed.

- **Romans 10:13 For whosoever shall call upon the name of the Lord shall be saved.**

It is that basic. If you really want confirmation that God meant for it to be that basic, simply put your name in place of 'the world' in the verse below.

(John 3:16) "For God so loved the world, that he gave his only begotten Son, that whosoever believeth in him should not perish but have everlasting life."

It is my prayer that you have Christ to walk with you in this journey of life. We do not know what we will find along the way but He will be there with us if we let Him, ready to help us take a deep breath and use twelve foot pruners if necessary.

References

Spangler, Ann and Syswerda, Jean E. *Women of the Bible.* Grand Rapids, Michigan: Zondervan, 2007.

Acknowledgements

My husband knows me better than anyone and still loves me. He can read me like a book and it is his due to his encouragement over the years that I have now been able to achieve a dream of publishing one. Thank you, David for your loving support.

I thank my son for his acceptance of my dreams. You see, he doesn't enjoy reading or writing but he does understand the importance of pursuing dreams. Thanks DJ for 'making your own sandwich' on more than one occasion while I tapped away on my laptop.

Thanks to my parents, Bill and Mary Lou Harrell, for teaching me to always strive to do my best but more importantly to always do what is right.

One of the biggest blessings I have is the family that I became a part of on my wedding day. There isn't space (actually I can't afford) to list everyone here. This book is based upon events surrounding a family gathering. You all know who you are and I thank each of you for being such an important part of my life. Who knows what future events might get published...

There is one more special person who has been a huge source of encouragement even though she has only had a brief opportunity to assist me in this process. Thank you, Carol Schuck, my friend and co-worker for your editing skills and time. Your comments were the icing on my encouragement cake.

Author Biography

Theresa Harrell Hatfield has always had an affinity for writing. One of her dreams was to one day, have a published work. As she graduated high school and went into the work force, she pushed that dream to the back burner like many do. She married at the age of 20 and continued to work as an administrative assistant until she gave birth to her son DJ.

At that time, she opened her own business with an in-home daycare enjoying staying at home with her new baby and a few other children. She enjoyed teaching and mentoring these children and thought of writing children's books at that time; however with her busy schedule, she again, pushed that dream aside.

At the age of 40, her husband, David, bought her a laptop computer for her birthday, knowing of her dream of writing and hoping to fan the flames of creativity. Finally a writing contest through the Women of Faith tour got Theresa motivated to write this story.

During the 90's her husband was called into the ministry. Since that time she has led many ladies events and has spoken to many groups of ladies and teens. She has taught Sunday school and has been a wonderful helpmeet to her husband.

Theresa is married to her high school sweetheart and they, along with their son live in Avon, Indiana. She works as a senior administrative assistant at a community college and leads the Women of Excellence ministries at Harmony Baptist Church in Avon, IN, where her husband is Worship Pastor.